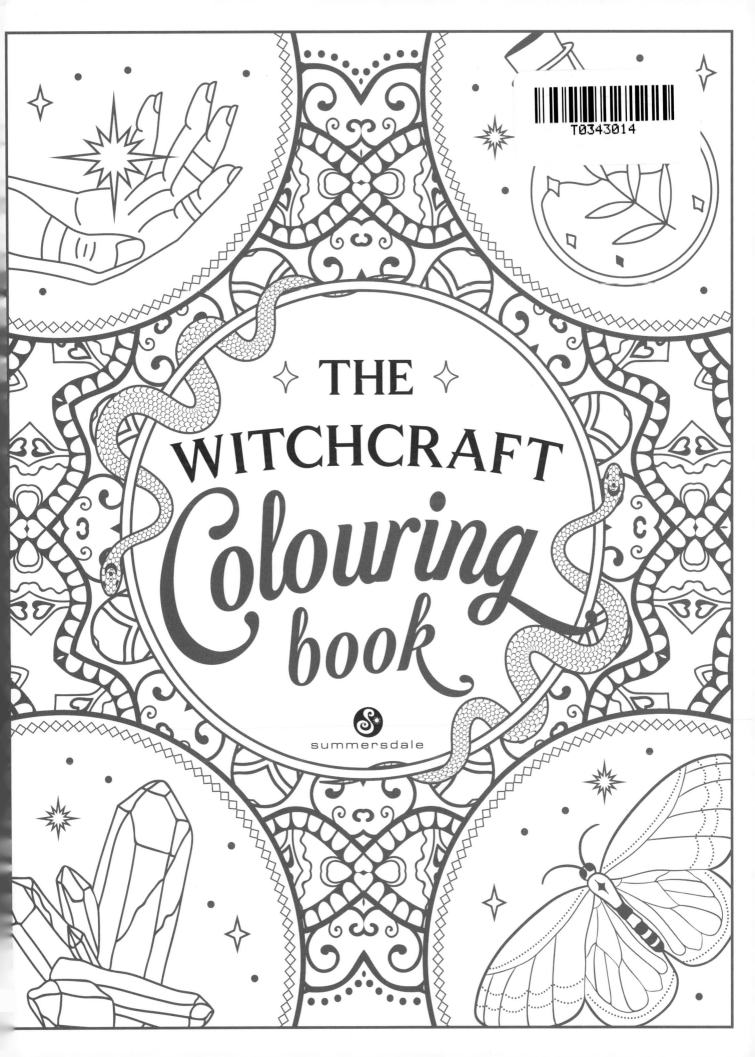

THE WITCHCRAFT COLOURING BOOK

Text by Holly Brook-Piper

An Hachette UK Company
www.hachette.co.uk

Summersdale Publishers Ltd
Part of Octopus Publishing Group Limited
Carmelite House
50 Victoria Embankment
LONDON
EC4Y 0DZ
UK

www.summersdale.com

Printed and bound in China

ISBN: 978-1-83799-206-5

Substantial discounts on bulk quantities of Summersdale books are available to corporations, professional associations and other organizations. For details contact general enquiries: telephone: +44 (0) 1243 771107 or email: enquiries@summersdale.com.

Disclaimer
Neither the author nor the publisher can be held responsible for any injury, loss or claim – be it health, financial or otherwise – arising out of the use, or misuse, of the suggestions made herein. This book is not intended as a substitute for the medical advice of a doctor or physician.

To..

From..

INTRODUCTION

Witchcraft is the practice of magick. The additional "k" differentiates the spiritual practice of magick from the stereotypical representations of stage magic.

Magick has been around for thousands of years, with some practices being traced back as far as early shamanism, and within this time it has endured a turbulent history. It wasn't until the 1950s, when the British law that prohibited witchcraft was repealed and Gerald Gardner published *The Gardnerian Book of Shadows*, that there was a resurgence in the practice and modern witchcraft was born. Since then, many different branches of the craft have emerged. While the term is often used interchangeably with "Wicca", not all witches are Wiccan, just as they are not all Pagan or Druid.

Due to widespread representations of levitation and elaborate spell-making, the word "witchcraft" can conjure up many stereotypical images where witches possess supernatural powers. This is not what witchcraft is about – rather, it is harnessing and aligning yourself with natural energies and redirecting them using your intentions to attain your deepest desires. This is commonly achieved through manifestation and performing spells and rituals.

With this book, you can step into the mystical world of modern witchcraft and discover this collection of striking illustrations that are ready to be brought to life with colour. Use this creative space to learn more about witchcraft while channelling your own magickal energies.

THE FIRST TIME I CALLED
MYSELF A "WITCH" WAS
THE MOST MAGICAL
MOMENT OF MY LIFE.

Margot Adler

WHITE WITCHCRAFT

White witchcraft helps you to connect with your inner power and harness the universe's natural energies, so you can achieve your hopes and dreams. By utilizing the power of the natural world, you can explore the magick within you. White witchcraft encourages both physical and emotional healing, reflection, self-care and self-discovery, and it can only be used for good, so there can be no malicious intent or call for harm upon yourself or others.

TYPES OF WITCH

There are a number of different types of practising witch:

Hedge witch – works with herbal magick

Kitchen witch – infuses cooking with magick, both with ingredients and intention

Elemental witch – calls upon the powers of earth, air, wind, water and fire

Cosmic witch – infuses celestial energy into their craft through astrology and astronomy

Secular witch – casts spells but doesn't believe their powers are spiritual

Eclectic witch – combines different traditions to form new ones

Green witch – is inspired by, and deeply connected to, nature

Solitary witch – practises alone

Sea witch – harnesses the power of the sea

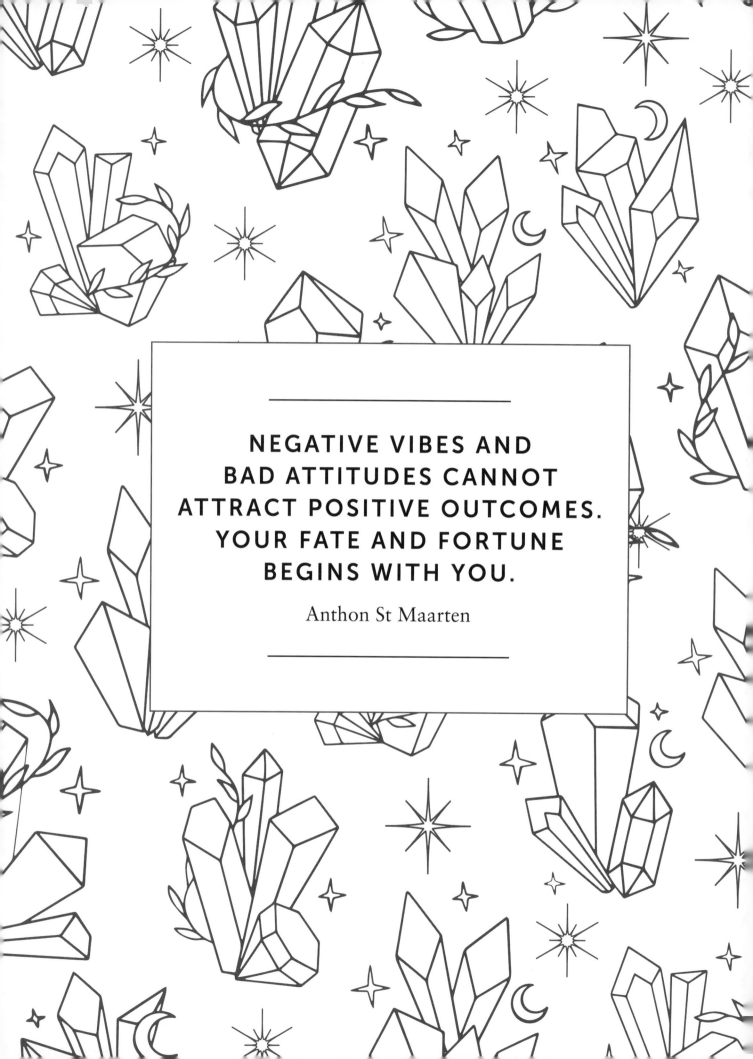

NEGATIVE VIBES AND
BAD ATTITUDES CANNOT
ATTRACT POSITIVE OUTCOMES.
YOUR FATE AND FORTUNE
BEGINS WITH YOU.

Anthon St Maarten

COVENS

A coven is the name given to a group
of witches who perform magick together.
You do not need to be in a coven to be a witch,
but it can be a good way to meet like-minded
souls. You may find that there isn't a witchy
fellowship in your area, in which case you
can look into virtual covens and connect
with others through social media.

NATURE

A reverence of nature lies at the heart of witchcraft. It is often viewed as the key to well-being and happiness and can teach you how to maintain balance and harmony in your life. By connecting to and drawing energy from nature, you can strengthen your connection to the universe, which results in you feeling empowered and enlightened. Many natural items, such as flowers, fruits and vegetables, are often used in witchcraft practices, as well as magickal props made from natural materials, like wands and besoms.

ALIGN WITH NATURE...
MAGIC HAPPENS.

John Friend

WAND

While self-empowerment is the most important
part of witchcraft, there are also tools that
can support witches in their practice.

Wands are popular due to their precision
in directing energy. They can be used to
consecrate a space, to call upon deities and
for basic divination. They are commonly
made from wood and are traditionally
fashioned from fallen tree branches.

The right wand will find you, so see what
catches your eye and use your intuition.

BELIEVE IN YOUR HEART
THAT YOU'RE MEANT TO
LIVE A LIFE FULL OF
PASSION, PURPOSE,
MAGIC AND MIRACLES.

Roy T. Bennett

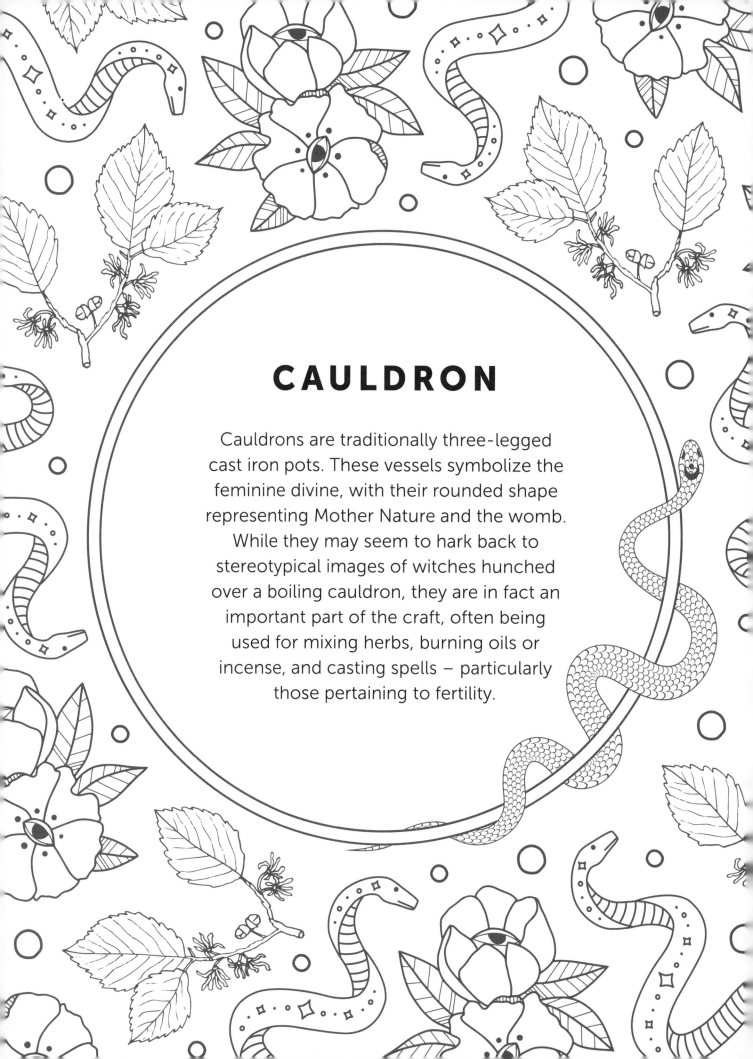

CAULDRON

Cauldrons are traditionally three-legged cast iron pots. These vessels symbolize the feminine divine, with their rounded shape representing Mother Nature and the womb. While they may seem to hark back to stereotypical images of witches hunched over a boiling cauldron, they are in fact an important part of the craft, often being used for mixing herbs, burning oils or incense, and casting spells – particularly those pertaining to fertility.

BROOM

While it may seem like a cliché, broomsticks –
traditionally called besoms – are still used in
modern witchcraft, although not for flight!
With bristles often fashioned out of birch twigs
and handles made from oak, broomsticks can
be used in cleansing rituals to sweep away
negative energy. They can also be placed
by your front door to protect against
these energies entering your home.

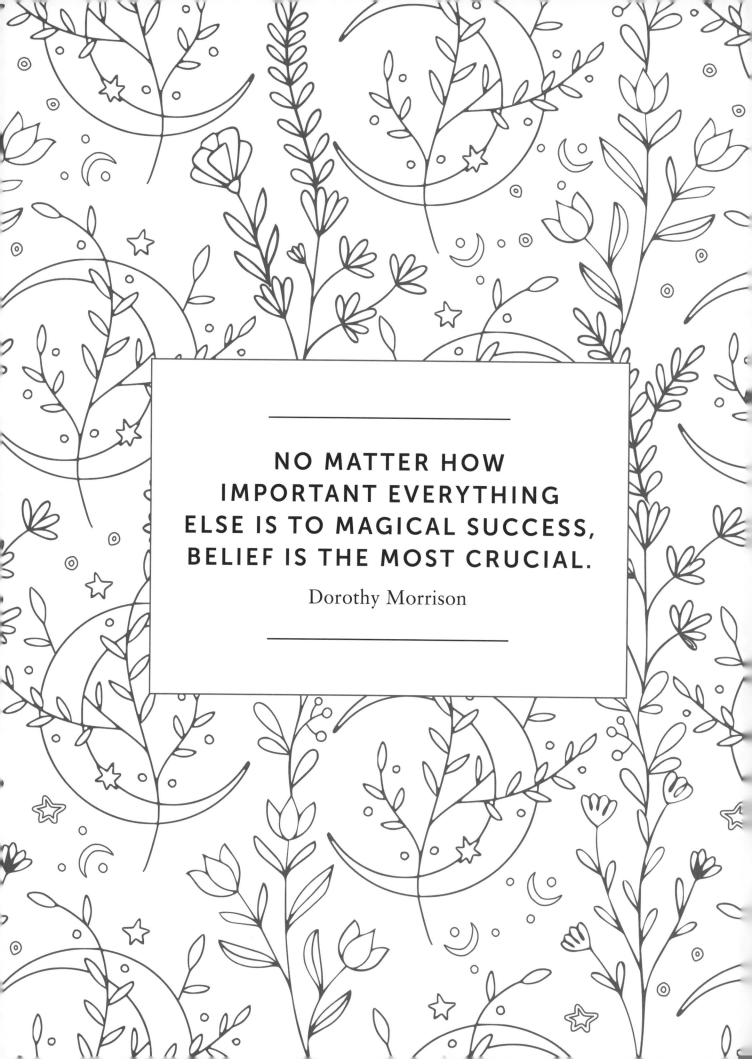

NO MATTER HOW IMPORTANT EVERYTHING ELSE IS TO MAGICAL SUCCESS, BELIEF IS THE MOST CRUCIAL.

Dorothy Morrison

GRIMOIRE

A grimoire is a magickal manual that details any information that may be of use to a witch. This can include instructions on how to perform spells, create magickal objects and summon spirits. In the past, grimoires have often been passed down through the generations. The origins of these spell books date back thousands of years, with archaeologists having discovered grimoires from the fifth century BCE.

ALTAR

An altar is a sacred space dedicated to practising magick. It doesn't have to be a large space; it can be a table, bookshelf or dresser. Decorate your altar with different witchcraft tools and symbols, such as crystals, statues, flowers and candles. You can redecorate your space to reflect different seasons or to honour specific deities. Before starting any magickal rituals, remember to cleanse your altar of any negative energy.

If you burn candles or incense at your altar, make sure they are kept away from anything flammable.

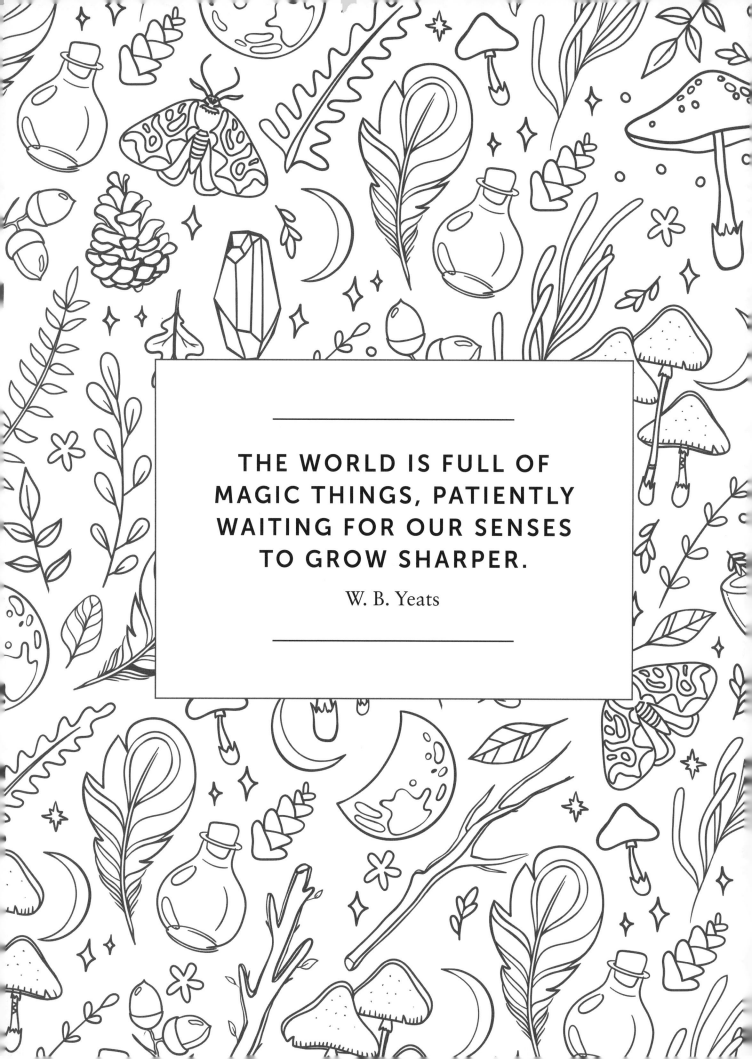

THE WORLD IS FULL OF
MAGIC THINGS, PATIENTLY
WAITING FOR OUR SENSES
TO GROW SHARPER.

W. B. Yeats

CANDLES

Candles are a popular tool used in modern magick. Focusing on the flame can help you to channel your intentions, assist you when tapping into your creativity and help you manifest your desires. They come in a wide variety of colours, scents, shapes and sizes, all of which have different associations. Because of their versatility, they can be used in a variety of different magickal practices, from spell work and rituals to connecting with your spiritual self.

TYPES OF CANDLE

Each candle colour has an "essence" that gives off a specific energy. Tailor your choice of candle to your intention.

White – protection, truth, peace

Red – strength, passion, attraction

Black – healing, banishing negativity

Green – luck, fertility, creativity

Yellow – clarity, happiness, success

Pink – fertility, friendship, beauty

Orange – positivity, courage

Blue – strength, healing, peace

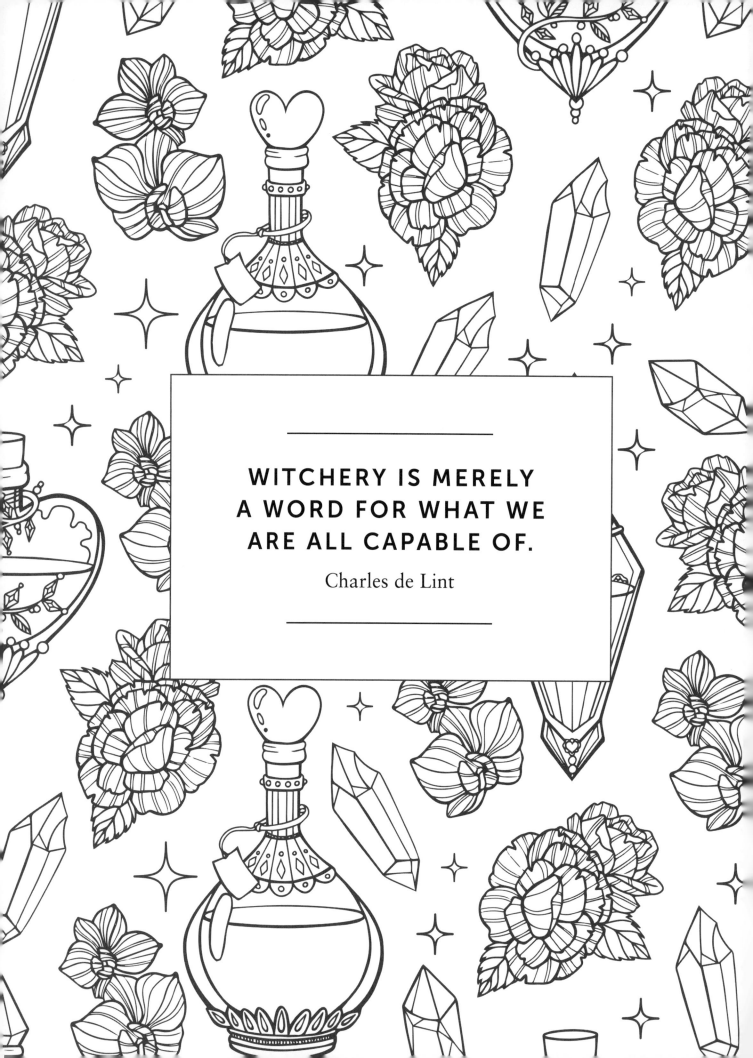

WITCHERY IS MERELY A WORD FOR WHAT WE ARE ALL CAPABLE OF.

Charles de Lint

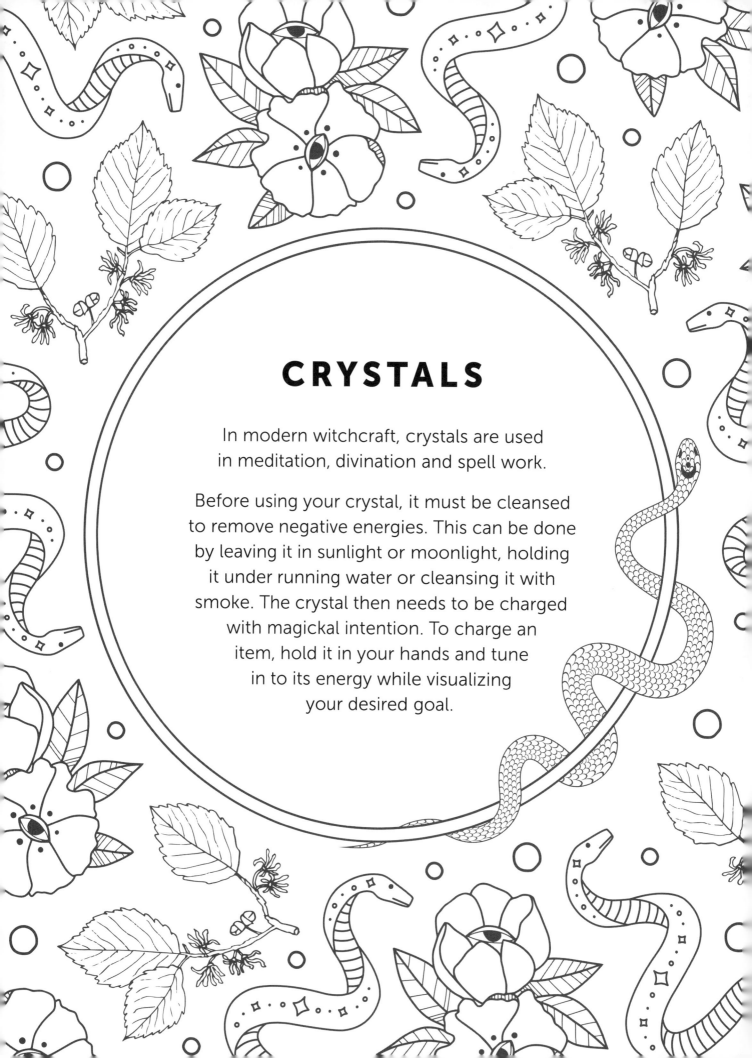

CRYSTALS

In modern witchcraft, crystals are used
in meditation, divination and spell work.

Before using your crystal, it must be cleansed
to remove negative energies. This can be done
by leaving it in sunlight or moonlight, holding
it under running water or cleansing it with
smoke. The crystal then needs to be charged
with magickal intention. To charge an
item, hold it in your hands and tune
in to its energy while visualizing
your desired goal.

TYPES OF CRYSTALS

Each type of crystal has its own unique spiritual properties. Match the type of stone you use to your intention. Some popular crystals include:

Agate – enhances perception and concentration, as well as instilling a sense of security

Amethyst – used for cleansing and consecrating a sacred space

Carnelian – wards off anything that is a drain on your mental and physical well-being

Clear quartz – one of the most versatile crystals; aids both physical and emotional healing

Jade – used to attain knowledge, specifically when resolving conflict

BEING A WITCH MEANS
LIVING IN THIS WORLD
CONSCIOUSLY, POWERFULLY
AND UNAPOLOGETICALLY.

Gabriela Herstik

HERBS

Herbs have a variety of uses in witchcraft because of their innate magickal properties. They are used to increase the potency of spells and rituals, can be burned to cleanse and charge magickal items, and can also be used as personal charms. It is believed that leaving herbs around your home banishes negative energy, promotes happiness and invites protection.

Always check any plants before you use them in magickal practices as there are some that are poisonous and must not be used.

SMOKE CLEANSING RITUAL

Smoke cleansing is where dried herbs are bundled up and burned to banish negative energies from spaces and magickal items. Each herb has its own magickal properties, so match the herb to your intention when smoke cleansing.

Rosemary – protection, purification

Bay – protection, success, good fortune

Sage – good luck, wisdom

Camomile – tranquillity, sleep, inner peace

Lavender – love, peace, tranquillity

Oregano – money, love, joy

Basil – wealth, prosperity, luck

When burning herbs, always keep a bowl of water close by so you can submerge the burning herbs quickly if necessary. Do not perform these rituals around children or pets.

THERE ARE BEAUTIFUL
MOMENTS OF MAGIC
IN EVERYONE'S LIFE.

Penélope Cruz

THE PENTAGRAM

A pentagram is one of the most recognizable symbols used in the practice of witchcraft. The distinctive five-pointed star is a protective symbol, commonly placed anywhere requiring protection. (It should not be mistaken for a pentacle: a five-pointed star enclosed within a circle, which traditionally represents the elements.) A pentagram can be worn as jewellery to shield the wearer from harm or placed within the home to drive away unwanted energies.
It can also be used in magickal spell work.

SIGILS

Sigils are symbols that hold magickal or mystical
meaning. In modern witchcraft, "sigil" refers
to a magickal intention that is condensed into
a single image and used to manifest desires.
These images can be a combination of symbols,
colours and codes. Creating a unique sigil to
represent your intention can be a powerful
way to express your wish to the universe
while also maintaining privacy, because
its symbolism is known only to you.

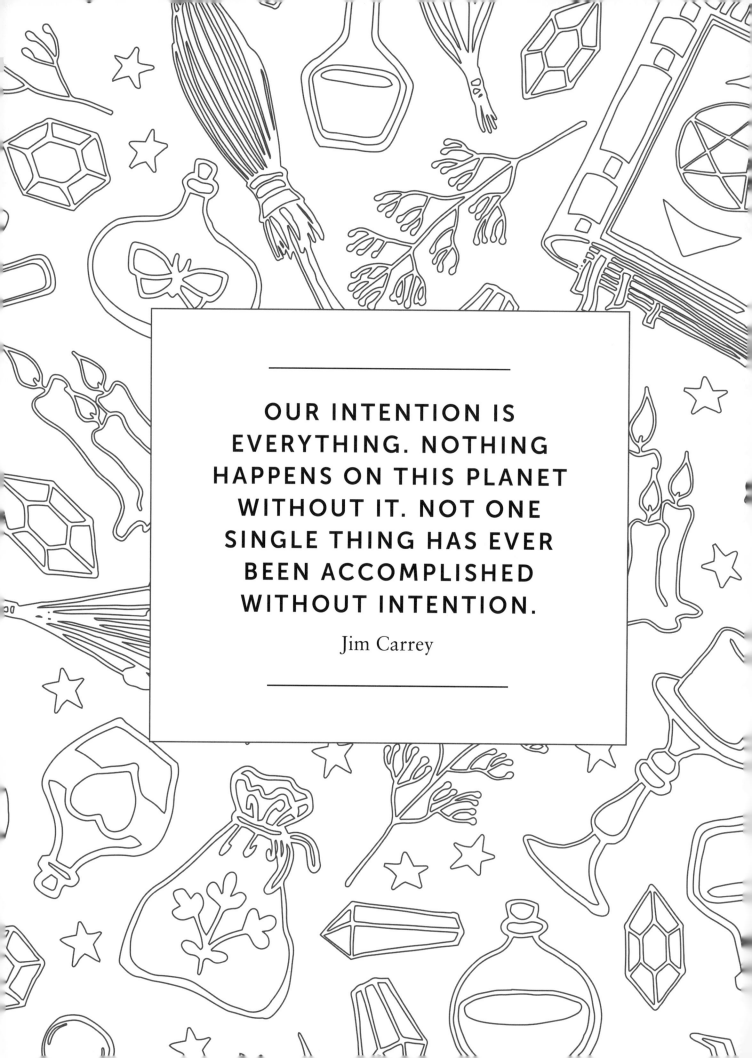

OUR INTENTION IS
EVERYTHING. NOTHING
HAPPENS ON THIS PLANET
WITHOUT IT. NOT ONE
SINGLE THING HAS EVER
BEEN ACCOMPLISHED
WITHOUT INTENTION.

Jim Carrey

MEDITATION

Meditation has become a key part of modern witchcraft. Many witches choose to perform this ancient practice before spellcasting or manifesting as it allows them to connect with the universe at a higher level and to be more in tune with their surroundings. It can also help to communicate your dreams and desires to deities. Try meditating for 15 minutes before performing any spells or rituals for the best results.

MANIFESTATION

Manifestation is about directing your positive energy towards a specific desired outcome and calling upon the universe to assist you in your endeavours.

To manifest, visualize your intention or goal, and envisage yourself in that life. Make sure you are viewing your desired life from your perspective and include as much detail as possible: consider all five of your senses – what can you see, touch, hear, smell and taste?

ASK FOR WHAT
YOU WANT AND BE
PREPARED TO GET IT.

Maya Angelou

DIVINATION

Divination isn't about seeing into the future. Instead, it offers solutions and insight to questions or problems. Common divination practices include:

Rune casting – uses an ancient alphabet that can help focus your mind on a particular problem

Tarot reading – uses a set of cards that provide insight through interpretation of its symbolism

Astrology – studies the zodiac and how it affects everyday life

Pendulum dowsing – uses a weighted object that moves independently to answer a "yes" or "no" question

DEITIES

Deities are divine beings who can communicate through meditation, spellcasting and rituals. Working with deities in your witchcraft practice can bring an added spiritual touch. Connecting with these spiritual beings is very much a personal decision; let your intuition guide your choice of gods or goddesses. Popular deities include the god and goddess from Wicca witchcraft: the Triple Goddess and the Horned God.

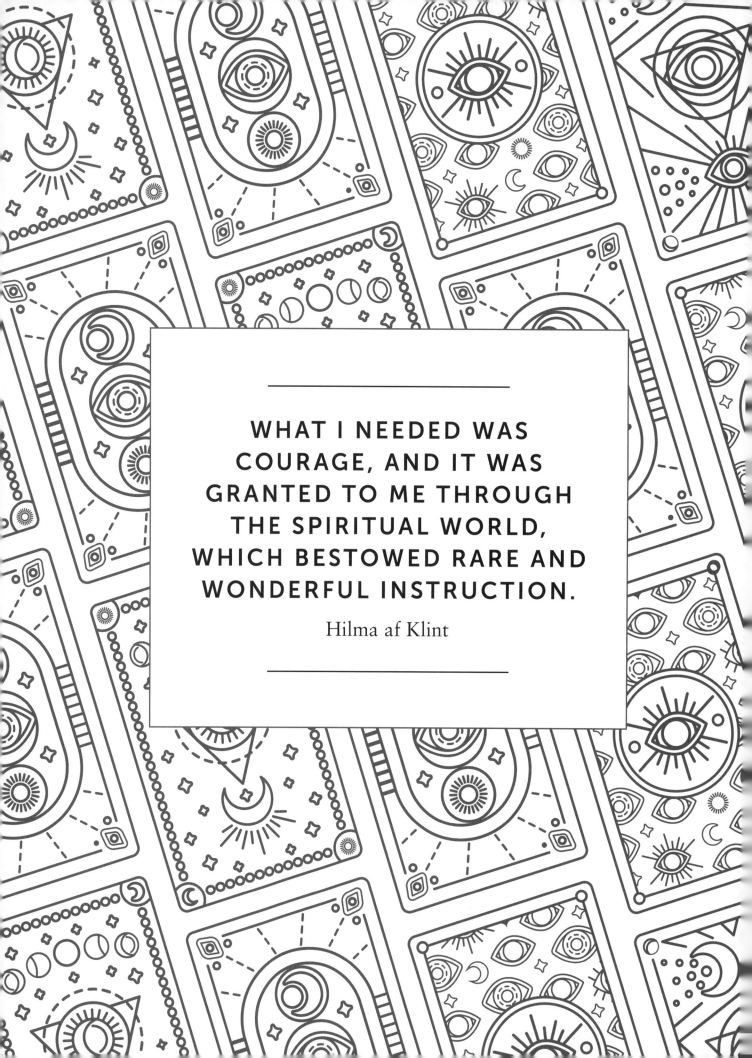

WHAT I NEEDED WAS
COURAGE, AND IT WAS
GRANTED TO ME THROUGH
THE SPIRITUAL WORLD,
WHICH BESTOWED RARE AND
WONDERFUL INSTRUCTION.

Hilma af Klint

SEASONAL CELEBRATIONS

Witches celebrate certain times of the year that centre around astronomical events. This annual cycle of seasonal festivities is called the Wheel of the Year and it charts the eight Sabbats (festivals). The most notable of these are the summer and winter solstices and the spring and autumn equinoxes. These four solar events are often referred to as "quarter days" and the midpoints between them are known as "cross-quarter days", or "fire festivals".

THE MOON

Many witches cast their spells in accordance with the moon's cycles as each phase has different lunar energy. By connecting your intentions to the lunar cycle, your spells can be even more effective.

New moon – the best time for spells that herald new beginnings and positive change, such as love spells

Waxing moon – advantageous for spells inviting growth, such as abundance spells

Full moon – the most powerful time for magick, so cast your spells wisely

Waning moon – the best time for spells that cast out negative forces, such as repulsion spells

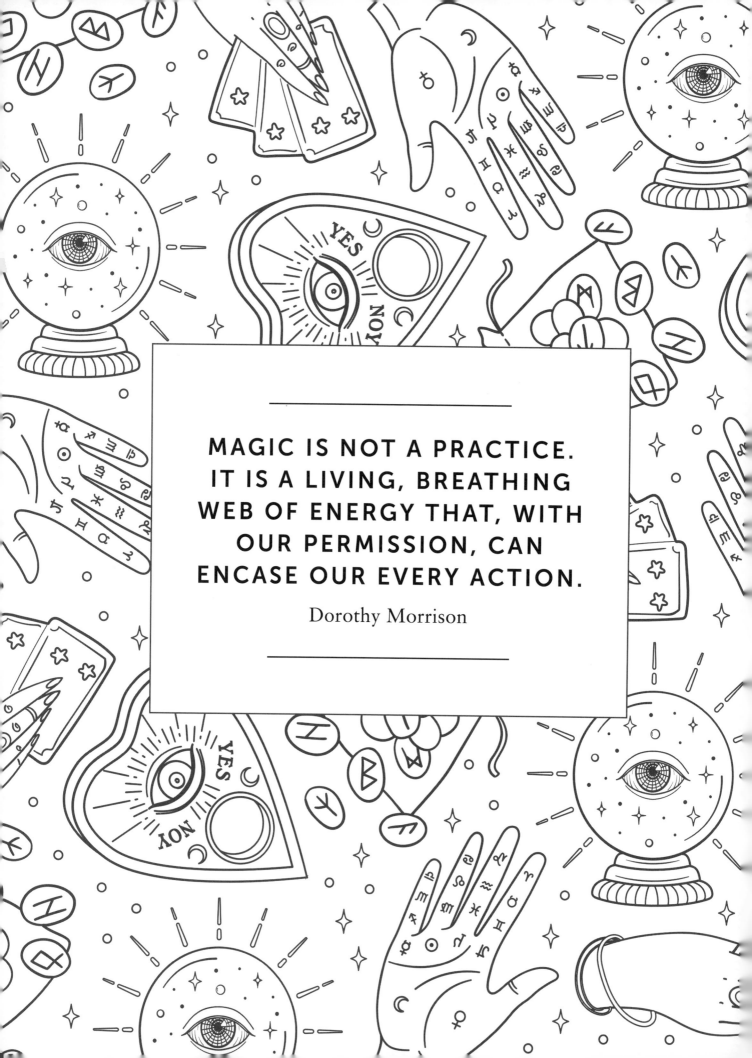

MAGIC IS NOT A PRACTICE.
IT IS A LIVING, BREATHING
WEB OF ENERGY THAT, WITH
OUR PERMISSION, CAN
ENCASE OUR EVERY ACTION.

Dorothy Morrison

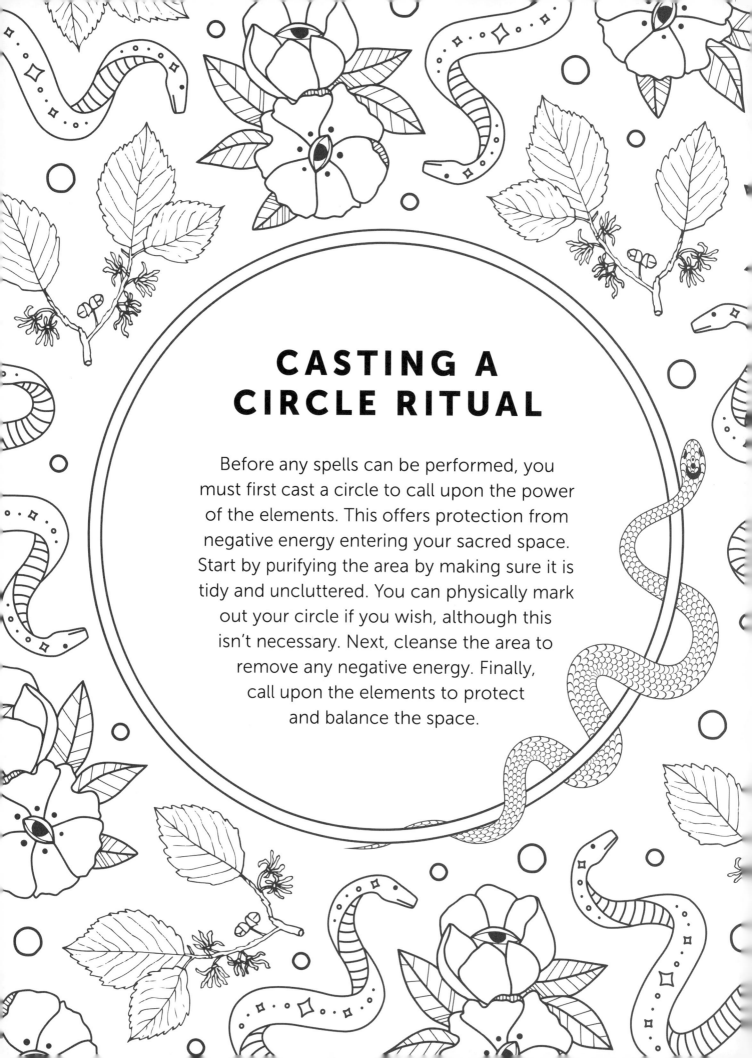

CASTING A CIRCLE RITUAL

Before any spells can be performed, you must first cast a circle to call upon the power of the elements. This offers protection from negative energy entering your sacred space. Start by purifying the area by making sure it is tidy and uncluttered. You can physically mark out your circle if you wish, although this isn't necessary. Next, cleanse the area to remove any negative energy. Finally, call upon the elements to protect and balance the space.

BEING A WITCH GIVES YOU
THE POWER TO HEAL YOURSELF,
CHANGE YOUR LIFE, CHANGE
YOUR WORLD AND CONJURE
YOUR EVERY DREAM.

Juliet Diaz

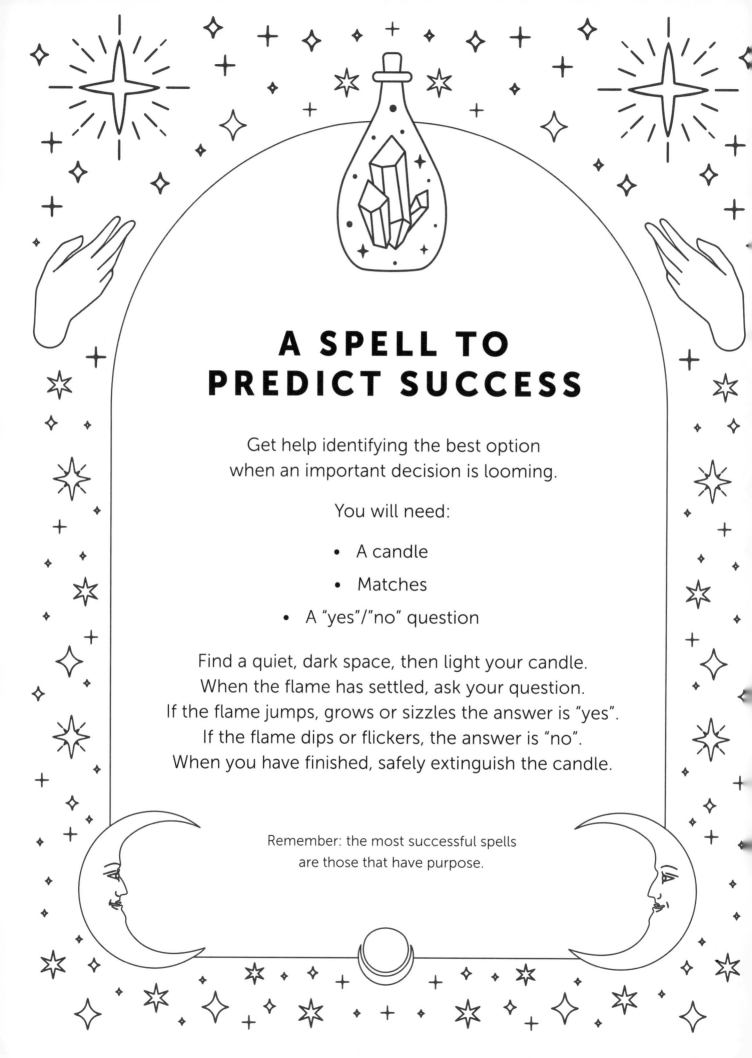

A SPELL TO PREDICT SUCCESS

Get help identifying the best option
when an important decision is looming.

You will need:

- A candle
- Matches
- A "yes"/"no" question

Find a quiet, dark space, then light your candle.
When the flame has settled, ask your question.
If the flame jumps, grows or sizzles the answer is "yes".
If the flame dips or flickers, the answer is "no".
When you have finished, safely extinguish the candle.

Remember: the most successful spells
are those that have purpose.

A SPELL FOR PROTECTION FROM THE EVIL EYE

Defend yourself from the gaze of the evil eye and its effects, including brain fog and bad luck.

You will need:

- A white bowl filled with 500 ml (1 pint) of water
- 50 ml (3 tbsp) olive oil
- Scissors
- Two garlic bulbs

Drip oil off your little finger into water. If the oil scatters you are fine, but if it gathers into a glob the evil eye is upon you. Break the spell with a release prayer while snipping the scissors over the bowl. Repeat the entire process as necessary. When you are free, place the garlic at your front and back door.

Cast this spell at a time of emotional strength. If powered by stress, expect an erratic outcome.

MAGIC IS JUST SCIENCE THAT WE DON'T UNDERSTAND YET.

Arthur C. Clarke

A SPELL FOR HAPPINESS

Bring on the feel-good vibes with this personal happiness spell.

You will need:

- A piece of yellow cloth
- 1 tbsp of honey
- A hawthorn tree

During the night of a full moon, sit close to your hawthorn tree and connect to its energy. Take your cloth and pierce it onto one of the tree's thorns, chanting, "Spirit of the hawthorn tree, bring happiness to me."

When casting a spell, always make sure your intention focuses on the positive.

A SPELL FOR LOVE

A spell to encourage love; new or existing.

You will need:

- Red or pink jewellery
- A herb of your choosing
- Romantic music
- Candles

Purify your space by burning your candle, then smoke-cleanse your jewellery by burning your chosen herb. Play romantic music to create the perfect ambiance. Hold your jewellery in both hands and visualize your desires. Slip on the jewellery and close the spell by saying, "And so it will be."

Be patient; sometimes things take time.

LOVE FOR LIFE IN ALL
ITS FORMS IS THE BASIC
ETHIC OF WITCHCRAFT.

Starhawk

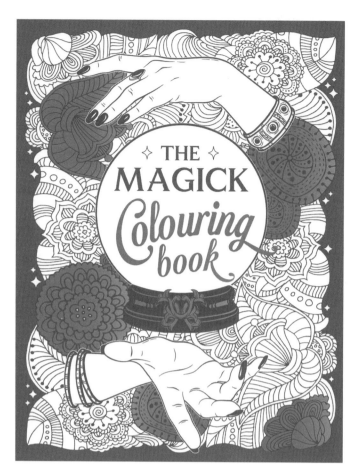

THE MAGICK COLOURING BOOK

A Spellbinding Journey of Colour and Creativity

Paperback

ISBN: 978-1-80007-404-0

Embark on a bewitching journey into the world of magick with this collection of intricate and striking images, ready for you to colour and complete as you wish. Featuring enchanted creatures, mystical objects and a host of other esoteric miscellanea, this colouring book offers an array of beautiful designs to celebrate the beliefs and practices associated with the supernatural world.

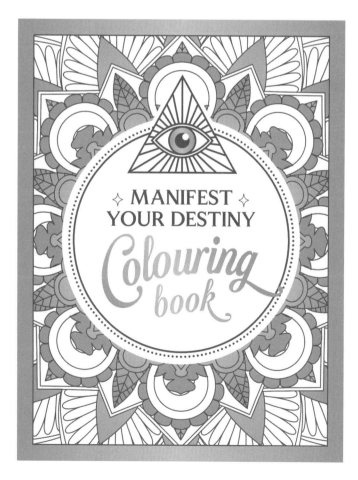

MANIFEST YOUR DESTINY COLOURING BOOK

A Mesmerizing Journey of Colour and Creativity

Paperback

ISBN: 978-1-80007-924-3

Discover the secret to manifesting your dreams with these pages, full of enchanting images and helpful guidance. These intricate patterns will help boost your creativity, raise your vibrations and ultimately support you on your manifesting journey. So relax, and let the universe guide you.

THE TAROT COLOURING BOOK

A Mystical Journey of Colour and Creativity

Paperback

ISBN: 978-1-83799-083-2

Step into the spiritual world of Tarot and seek insight into your past, present and future while awakening your creativity with these striking illustrations. Within this bewitching colouring book you will find Tarot-themed images alongside essential details about the meanings of the cards, and how to interpret their symbolism and understand your Tarot readings.

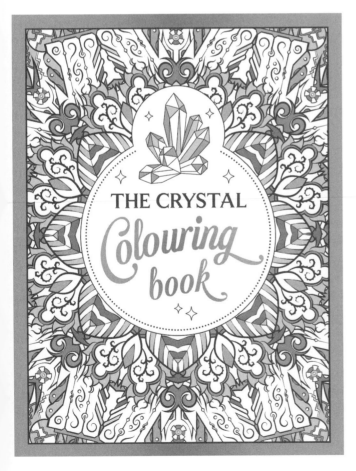

THE CRYSTAL COLOURING BOOK

A Healing Journey of Colour and Creativity

Paperback

ISBN: 978-1-83799-084-9

Immerse yourself in the spiritual world of crystals and bring this striking collection of images to life with colour. Begin a voyage of self-discovery and creativity while learning what it is about crystals that has seen them treasured and admired throughout history.

Have you enjoyed this book?

If so, find us on Facebook at **Summersdale Publishers**, on Twitter at **@Summersdale**
and on Instagram and TikTok at @summersdalebooks and get in touch.

We'd love to hear from you!

www.summersdale.com

IMAGE CREDITS